STEPHEN AK

The
Mobile
Millionaire

Making the Most of
Mobile Technology

The
Mobile
Millionaire

Making the Most of
Mobile Technology

By

STEPHEN AKINTAYO

THE MOBILE MILLIONAIRE

Copyright ©2015 by Stephen Akintayo

All rights reserved.

■

Stephen Akintayo asserts the moral right to be identified as the author of this book.

■

ISBN-13:978-1517139902

ISBN-10:1517139902

Published in Nigeria By:
Gtext Media
www.gtext.com
gtextgroup@gmail.com
(+234) 8188220077, 8188220066, 08188111999
23, Ajayi Road, Oke-Ira, Ogba,
Lagos State.
In Partnership With:
Seradia Brooks Limited
seradiabrooks.com
seradiabrooks@gmail.com
+23498169126032
Cover Designed by:
Ojo Timothy [deluxedesignsvilla@gmail.com]

THIS PAGE
WAS LEFT BLANK
INTENTIONALALLY

Table of Contents ─────────

THE MOBILE MILLIONAIRE

MOBILE TECHNOLOGY: HISTORY AND EVOLUTION

Mobile technology has rapidly evolved through the years. Having once being the privilege of a few, it is now accessible to world over at an affordable rate. At one time it was needed for long-distance communication and used just for conversations. Now it serves a plethora of functions which can be easily handled while on the go; activities which include talking, sending messages, listening to the radio or music, watching films, sending of emails, marketing, etc.

With the evolution has come a transformation in the size of mobile devices. From being gargantuan to being small enough to fit in your palm, mobile phones have indeed come a long way. Having witnessed its transformation in the last seventy years, be thankful yours fits in your pocket. Maybe one day it will even be able to bend like a piece of thin plastic. Maybe you won't even have to touch it, doing all of your multitasking from cellular implants. But seventy years ago, lugging a 25-pound 'portable' phone on your back, with very limited 5-mile range, was the norm.

Let's go back in time a little bit to understand changes experienced in the mobile world.

A BRIEF HISTORY

1938

Not quite what you would consider a mobile phone, the SCR-194 and 195 were the first portable AM radios, produced by the U.S. Army Signal Corps Engineering Laboratories in Fort Monmouth, NJ. Considered the first "walkie talkie," these devices weighed roughly 25 pounds and had a 5-mile range. They were widely used for infantry battalion and company intercommunication during World War II.

1940

Next came the SCR-300 radio transceiver, developed for the U.S. Military by Motorola. This time a portable FM radio, it weighed anywhere from 32 to 38 pounds with a 3-mile range. It replaced the SCR-194 and 195 with nearly 50,000 units used in World War II by Allied Forces.

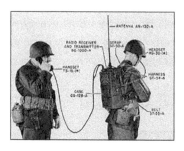

1942

Motorola produced the first "handie talkie" for the U.S., labelled SCR-536. 130,000 units were manufactured and used during the war. Back to AM, this handheld version shed the fat off the previous two transceivers, weighing only 5 pounds. But its land range was only 1-mile (3 miles over water). Moving away from military-grade portable radios, we get to the mobile radio telephones.

1946

Bell System introduced the first commercial mobile telephone service, called the Mobile Telephone System (MTS). The original equipment was large, weighing 80 pounds (not quite what you'd call mobile) with limited calling bands available from AT&T. The service wasn't cheap either—costing $30 a month (roughly $330 today) with additional per call charges. Not really intended for regular Joe Blows, these devices were used by utilities, truck fleet operators, and reporters.

1956

Ericsson's Mobile System A (MTA) was the first partly automatic mobile system for automobiles. First used by Sweden, the unit weighed a whopping 88 pounds. Again, "mobile" is kind of a misnomer, considering it is equivalent to almost 300 iPhones!

1964

With the adaption of Bell's newer pre-cellular Improved Mobile Telephone Service (IMTS), auto owners saw lighter, more advanced mobile car phones with push buttons. This one by Motorola weighed 40 pounds, half as much of the original units from the '40s. Over the years, they managed to get down into the 20-pound range. But they never managed to get into the hands of Joe Blow, with a still-hefty price and rationed service throughout the nation.

1973

With a prototype of the DynaTAC (DYNamic Adaptive Total Area Coverage) portable phone, former Motorola Vice President Martin Cooper made the first private, practical mobile phone call in a non-vehicle setting. Who would he call? His rival at Bell Labs, Joel S. Engel.

1982

With the impressive size of the DynaTAC prototype, it's disappointing to see Nokia's Mobira Senator weighing in at 22 pounds. It launched during the world's first fully automatic international cellular service—NMT—the first- generation (1G) of mobile communications.

1983

10 years later after the prototype, Motorola's Dyna-TAC cellular phone was made available to the public, weighing under 2 pounds, but costing nearly $4,000 (almost $9,000 today)—which is why it was strictly for the Gordon Gekkos of the world. It worked on AMPS, North America's first 1G analog service, launched first by Ameritech in Chicago.

1984

Back to larger mobile devices, the Mobira Talkman brought longer talk time at cheaper costs. The DynaTAC could only manage 60 minutes of talk time, but this miniature beast gave hours or voice- to-voice communication

1989

Next up was Motorola's MicroTAC, which introduced the first flip phone design. The hardware was place in a hinged section of the phone, reducing the phone's size when not in use. It was truly the world's first pocket phone.

1992

The Motorola International 3200 became the first hand-sized digital mobile phone that used 2G digitally en-crypted technology (unveiled in 1991 as GSM).

1993

Perhaps the world's first smartphone, IBM Simon

was a mobile phone, pager, fax machine and PDA, all rolled into one. It included a calendar, address book, clock, calculator, notepad, email, gamers and a touchscreen with QWERTY keyboard. It originally sold for $899, which would be just over $1,300 nowadays. You may remember Simon from Sandra Bullock's The Net.

1994

Car phones remained popular, despite their smaller pocket- sized versions, but Motorola's Bag Phone (2900) was the car phone to have due to its long talk time, great battery life and superior signal range. They first worked with 1G networks, but eventually crossed over into 2G territory.

1996

Still shrinking the line of TACs, Motorola unveiled the first clamshell mobile phone with StarTAC. It improved the

folding feature by collapsing in half, which is why it's called "clamshell"—because it resembles a clam opening and closing shut. It ran on 1G networks, but eventually crossed over into the world of 2G. It's said to be inspired by the communicator from the original Star Trek series.

1997

The Simon was good, but the Nokia 9000 Communicator was what really brought on the smartphone era. It was the first cell phone that could also be called a mini-computer (though it had limited web access). When opened, the longways clamshell design revealed an LCD screen and full *QWERTY* keyboard—the first on a mobile phone.

1998

The Nokia 8810 was the first cell phone without an external antenna whip or stub-antenna, possibly paving the way for iPhones and DROIDs. It also made mobile phones more aesthetically pleasing, with its sliding keypad cover.

1999

One of the most popular mobile phones in history was the Nokia 3210, with over 160 million sold. It was one of the first to allow picture messages, but only preinstalled ones like "Happy Birthday" and was one of the first to be marketing toward young people.

1999

Nokia's 7110 was the first cell phone to incorporate Wireless Application Protocol (WAP), which gave mobile users web access for simple devices—a stripped-down, mostly text version, but a revolutionary step for mobile internet.

1999

GeoSentric was responsible for the world's first mobile phone and a GPS navigator integrated in one product—the Benefon Esc! It was splashproof, greyscale, and allowed users to load maps to trace position and movement.

1999

In Japan, Kyocera's Visual Phone (VP-201) was the first to have a built-in camera, but it was designed primarily as a peer-to-peer video phone, as opposed to Sharp's the next

year...

2000

Sharp was first to the camera phone market with their J-SH04 (J-Phone), released by J-Mobile in Japan. It offered a mere0.1 megapixel resolution. Some like to give credit to Olympus for being the first camera to transmit digital images over a cellular network with their Deltis VC-1100. Others prefer Philippe Kahn's story of rigging up a camera to a cell phone with wires to send images of his newborn baby.

But the J-SH04 was the first commercially available cell phone to have an integrated CCD sensor, with the Sha-Mail (Picture-Mail) infrastructure. This was the start of what we know as MMS.

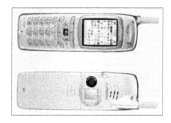

2002

Not too far from the J-Phone, the Sanyo 5300 from Sprint was the first camera phone sold in North America.

2002

RIM's BlackBerry 5810 wasn't the first BlackBerry device, but it was the first to incorporate a mobile phone into their popular brand of data-only devices.

Professionals who needed immediate access to their emails and schedules were the main target for RIM, but the built-in phone made it appealing to everyone. The downside? No speaker or microphone.

2002

One of the first phones to equip a fully functional web experience and integrate an instant messaging client (AIM) was the Danger Hiptop in 2002, later re-branded the T- Mobile Sidekick.

Its messaging features and keyboard made it one of the best selling phones in the deaf community. Also new was an

LCD screen that rotated and flipped to reveal a large QW-ERTY keyboard.

2002

Perhaps surpassing the BlackBerry achievements, Microsoft's Pocket PC Phone Edition started spreading across PDAs like wildfire, including the HP Jornada 928 Wireless Digital Assistant, combining the best of the PDA with integrated wireless voice and data capabilities.

It was a nice addition to the older Windows Mobile Classic devices, which essential ran a mini-version of Windows XP.

2002

Another PDA adding phone support was Palm's Treo 180 by Handspring, running the Palm OS.

2004

The next highly popular device was a camera phone called the Motorola RAZR, which was first marketed as a "fashion" phone in 2004, selling 50 million units by mid-2006.

It helped give cell phones a new look, which were getting stale with the same ol' boring designs. Though nothing revolutionary, its looks did more than impress.

2005

The first Palm smartphone to operate outside of the Palm OS was the Treo 700w, powered by Windows Mobile. It was a great alternative for users who needed access to Microsoft software on the go.

2005

Believe it or not, the iPhone wasn't the first cell phone to have Apple's iTunes music player integrated. It was the Motorola ROKR E1, but it only could manage 100 songs at a time—not quite the same as an iPhone.

2007

In 2007, Steve Jobs introduced the Apple iPhone, a revolutionary touchscreen smartphone. It wasn't the first smartphone, but it was the first to get the user interface right, eventually adapting 3G technology (which was already available since 2001).

2008

The first smartphone to run Google's Android OS was the HTC Dream slider smartphone. It featured a QWERTY keyboard, full HTML web browser, Gmail, YouTube and more, and paved the way for phones like the Nexus One and Motorola DROID.

2010

The HTC EVO 4G from Sprint was the first cellular phone to meet 4G standards, running on the WiMAX network. It was sold powered by Android 2.1 and had one of the largest touchscreen displays, an 8MP camera, HD video capture, HDMI output, Mobile Hotspot capability and HTC Sense.

Over the past few years, the demand for smart-phones has grown exponentially as companies develop increasingly advanced software and features. Popular mobile phone apps have truly revolutionized the entire mobile phone industry.

Smart-phones are defined as mobile telephone devices boasting PC-like functionality and featuring powerful processors, open operating systems, vast memory capabilities, and the ability to interface with built-in features such as miniature *QWERTY* keyboards, touch screens, cameras, contact management programs, GPS or navigation hardware, media software for playing or storing music, and internet connectivity.

The first mobile device categorized as a "smart-phone" appeared on the market in 1993, as a product called Simon, designed by IBM and carried by Bell South. Simon featured an on-screen keyboard, a calendar, world clock, calculator, address book, e-mail and facsimile capabilities and games.

While these programs would seem simple by today's standards, Simon was certainly the first phone of its kind, and set the precedent for phones such as the BlackBerry, released in 2001 and the iPhone, released in 2007.

MOBILE TECHNOLOGY TODAY

Today's consumer is a different animal compared to those of previous generations. We want our information when we want it, and in a certain format. Furthermore, we use a different array of devices to access all this information and want it uniform across all platforms. This makes it very difficult to determine how best to get a consumers attention.

Current trends show us that people are migrating from the traditional Desktop/laptop to their mobile devices for their primary computing needs. This trend is increasing at brisk pace due to lifestyle changes; people are not confined to the desk for work due to the fact that they can multitask and take their work onto their mobile devices.

With mobile penetration being at such a high percentage production of mobile phone and its sale can be exploited to keep up to date with consumer's needs and demands. Having provisions for relevant content to this key demographic will be vital and remain viable in this dynamic environment. This opens up numerous avenues to make it in the mobile technology sector.

A few mobile device companies are listed below showing how well they have penetrated the U.S. market. Presently,

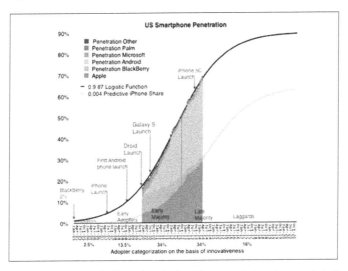

based on the graph, Google's Android currently has larger global mobile penetration closely followed by Apple's IOS; this slight advantage due to having a variety of staggered products targeting different demographics of the market being licensed to different manufactures has allowed Google the concentrate on its core operating system. This has eroded operating systems such as Palm & Blackberry almost rendering them obsolete. Thus making the environment saturated with android devices.

To remain relevant companies must use this early advantage to good use and further diversify into other niche segments of techno savvy individuals. Below are a few examples of ways, beyond the sale of mobile devices, that companies can make big money in this sector.

The Growth Of Mobile Applications

Application software for smart phones have changed the way we interact with our mobile phones. These apps have driven the growth of mobile technology to a larger extent and keep evolving to suit our personal needs.

This sector has grown into a billon dollar industry and in the European Union alone over 500 000 jobs have been attributed to the developing of apps. Further more, businesses have identified the importance of having tailor-made apps that are particular to their organizations. The importance of these mobile apps can now be likened to having a website; any organization meaning to stay relevant must have an app; anyone wanting to make it in the mobile technology sector should definitely have some form of presence in either the development, distribution and usage of apps.

Mobile Accessories

Our mobile devices are now personalized in relation to our individual preferences to a large extent, thus making this industry big business; covers, skins, screen protection, and drop protection are all but a few of the products out there.

It is reported that smart phone accessories where valued at $20 billion in 2012. That's big money, and with the projected increase of the use of these devices the figures speak for themselves.

Mobile Apps

To make money online, it is important that you know where your market is. Then you can craft your marketing activities to reach your potential customers. It should be known that marketing is a game of numbers. The more your reach, the more your response rate (provided you get your homework right).

I present to you in this chapter the top ten (10) commonly used apps on mobile devices.

Popular mobile phone apps (an abbreviation for 'applications') have become the next craze amongst smart-phone users. Mobile service providers now offer a vast array of applications that can be downloaded directly onto smart-phones. The App Store, launched by Apple Inc., has become

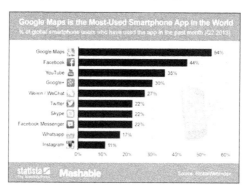

the most widely recognized application service, offering both free and paid applications that can be downloaded directly to the iPhone, iPod and iPad, through Apple's iTunes store. Curious about applications for Smartphones? Begin by browsing Apple's App Store, or the online BlackBerry App World catalogue. Here is a list of the most popular mobile phone apps and mobile phone app categories.

Top Ten Most Popular Mobile-Phone App Categories

1. **Voice Command/Voice-Control** - A variety of popular mobile apps for smart-phones have made it easier to use voice commands to look up contacts, dial phone calls by voice command, dictate e-mail or text messages, select music, or even browse websites or television stations by voice control, without pressing any buttons.

2. **MobiTV** - This application offers both television and digital radio stations to mobile phones. MobiTV stations include MSNBC, ABC News, ESPN, CNN, CSPAN, The Weather Channel, The Discovery Channel, etc.

3. **Skype** - anyone interested in saving cell phone minutes or reducing the cost of international phone calls is sure to praise Skype, a high quality application for free Skype-to-Skype long distance calls over WiFi.

4. **Games** have ranked as some of the most popular applications offered through Apple's App Store. In 2009, Apple announced their list of the year's most highly purchased games, titles which ranged in price from Vivendi Games' Crash Bandicoot Nitro Cart 3D, $5.99, to Texas Hold 'Em, $4.99, to Freeverse's Moto Chaser, priced at $.99. Other popular games range from role playing games to strategy, puzzles, word games and card games.

5. **Social Networking Apps** such as Facebook, Twitter, and LinkedIn, Loopt, and Hey Where Are You? are

steadily climbing toward the top of the list of downloadable applications for smart-phones.

6. Productivity applications for smart-phones are highly praised for helping tech savvy users to keep their lives organized. Popular mobile phone apps to increase productivity include To Do Lists, The StockWatch, PageOnce Personal Assistant, Quote Sheets, Your Receipts Tracker, Attendance Countdown etc. There are even apps geared at youngsters and students, such as iStudiez Pro, which enables students to keep track of their class schedules, assignments, due dates, etc, all through the iPhone's touch-screen.

7. Search Tools have also been highly successful mobile apps; particularly search tools that capitalize on the GPS capabilities of smart-phones. Avoid typing in your current location, and use apps such as Urban Spoon to search for nearby restaurants, FourSquare or Yelp for information on local shopping, nightlife, entertainment, and even maps.

8. Financial tools - such as mobile bill pay and mobile banking have become popular applications for professionals on-the-go. The capabilities of these apps are projected to Increase in the future.

9. Mailing/Postal Services - UPS Mobile for iPhones and Androids allows users to print shipping labels, find UPS locations, estimate shipment costs, and delivery times, and track both incoming and outgoing shipping deliveries and packages.

10. Futuristic - Science Fiction fans will surely be fans of some of the latest, futuristic apps such as holographic images and projectors, augmented reality applications, interactivity and crowd sourcing and real time collaboration apps.

-

Uses Of Mobile Technology

The Autonomous Home

Imagine a scenario where you have a fully-fledged autonomous home that you can access through your phone? Sounds like something out of a Sci-Fi movie but this technology is available today to a niche market. Early adaptors in any environment will always have a head start and competitive edge when the rest of the market reacts to the new trends.

Being able to have access to one's home through an internet connection via their mobile phone or tablet is something that can keep Google a step ahead. This can be integrated through the Android operating system: switching the lights on, as well as setting the sprinklers, turning on the heating, as well as arming the alarm.

Big companies such as Sony are already developing home entertainment systems that can access the internet as well, controlling entertainment centres via Wi-Fi; so this is the right time to push through and have a Google based system that will make use of such developments

Small companies are already producing computerized home irrigation systems. Strategic partnerships with such small entrepreneurships would be a significant advantage to the early adapter. Furthermore funding such small start-ups will be like planting a seed for tomorrow.

Media

The average American spends 34 hours watching television. The entertainment industry is making tens of billions of dollars a year when Americans are making a second career out of their viewing habits. Recent lawsuits show us that the entertainment industry is worried. They are worried about the long-term threats presented by services like Hulu, Netflix, and especially YouTube.

YouTube was founded in 2005; and by 2007, 134 million Americans watched YouTube videos. Five years later, that number grew 37.3 percent to about 184 million Americans watching a video in any month of 2012. The increase in views and content length on YouTube presented a compelling opportunity for advertising.

Advertising

You can now target viewers with highly specific video ads by factors such as their location, age, income, sex, and interests; thus being in a much better position to see massive returns to your budget. Unlike with traditional TV advertising, 100% of your budget will reach the exact type of person you want. Companies are beginning to notice. YouTube alone made than $3.6 billion dollars last year. Demand has shifted from newspaper advertising, partly because the audience is shrinking, but mostly because of the compelling, well-targeted opportunities that digital advertising affords. Another big contributor in advertising on mobile platforms are mobile apps, these are racking in so much revenue and are a big opportunity.

E-commerce

Online retail is a booming industry. According to Forrester Research, it will grow by 14% this year alone. Companies like Amazon and eBay collapse have grown to massive sizes -- indicating the permanence of the market. This has given rise to mobile money or the mobile wallet. Banking services have had to adapt in this regard due to the rise of companies like PayPal. It's now so easy to use ones mobile phone to pay for services and goods.

The credit card is under threat from the emergence of mobile money or the mobile wallet. Instead of paying with cash or other traditional methods like debit cards, consumers now can use their mobile devices to make the transaction. This has further strengthened the value of the mobile platforms due to their ability to centralize services on one device. There is so much potential in this segment and growth is predicted to continue rising. In 2008 alone $600billion was spent using mobile money transactions.

Productivity

Microsoft made $21.592 billion dollars in revenue from Office last year, accounting for 65% of its operating income. Office is the company's most profitable arm - but one that is facing serious competition in the form of web based apps. These apps have changed how we do business in general. There are so many productivity apps out there to suit every need. The likes of Microsoft Office are facing a big challenge from these apps due to the fact that they are a lot cheaper and just as good.

While it's true that Microsoft Office currently dominates word processing with 95% of the market, major changes should occur in the area in the next 5 to 10 years. Much like the existence of Pepsi causes Coke prices to remain generally low -- the availability of these new productivity apps has forced the likes of Microsoft to radically reduce their prices, even as their cost is much higher than their competitors'

Gaming

In 2012, U.S. gaming companies made upwards of $14.8 billion dollars - a figure which is growing by 33% a year. Much of this revenue comes from mobile app sales. 75% of Google Play's revenue in the United States is generated by games. In places like South Korea, the figure is around the 95% mark. But gaming is increasingly developing core online features. Perhaps the earliest browser based game with mainstream success was RuneScape, which came out in 2001. It amassed more than 200 million users in a short time.

Following RuneScape came World of Warcraft, which peaked at 10 million paying subscribers and several billion dollars of revenue overall. Just like the app environment, games get most of their revenue for the use of target advertisements. The popularity of games like Candy Crush have reached near cult status, resulting in huge amounts of money pouring in, making the mobile tech environment a very lucrative area of focus. Social Facebook has fast developed a user base of more than 1.2 billion people. As humans we are inherently social creatures. Huge parts of our brains are developed for speech, facial recognition, and body language. It's natural for us to want to stay connected with those around us. This is the number one reason why we are constantly glued to our phones.

Whoever has the best or most popular social networking app is king. The likes of Whatsapp, Instagram, Twitter and Skype are making a killing in this regards. People want to be in touch with their peers, work mates, old school mates and loved ones.

The number one reason over 80% of people use their mobile device for now is social networking. Calling is now a secondary function of owning a mobile phone. It is now of paramount importance to have some sort of presence in this segment. As we are social beings, we are discussing our experiences in real time, and organizations have realized the importance of being present on social media, and how a simple mistake can make or break your brand these days.

TOOLS OF MOBILE MILLIONAIRES

A variety of tools are commonly used by many mobile millionaires the world over. We seek to explore a few.

Mobile Marketing

Mobile marketing is marketing on or with a mobile device, such as a Smartphone. It can provide customers with time and location sensitive, personalized information that promotes goods, services and ideas. Mobile (Digital) Marketing is a veritable tool both as a business and as business-promoting tool.

Personally, I make over Five Hundred Thousand Naira (Nigerian currency) each month doing mobile marketing (alone). It should be noted that mobile marketing can be both a business, and can also be a business-promoting tool.

31

This section seeks to explore some of the commonest mobile marketing platforms explored by mobile millionaires, of which I am a player too.

Mobile Adverts

This is a form of advertising via mobile (wireless) phones or other mobile devices. It is a subset of mobile marketing. Mobile advertising is targeted at mobile phones, a cost value that came estimably to a global total of 4.6 billion as of 2009. The emergence of this form of advertising is so real that there is now a dedicated global awards ceremony organized every year by Visiongain.

As mobile phones outnumber TV sets by over 3 to 1, and PC based internet users by over 4 to 1, and the total laptop and desktop PC population by nearly 5 to 1, advertisers in many markets have recently rushed to this media.

In Spain 75% of mobile phone owners receive ads, in France 62% and in Japan 54%. More remarkably as mobile advertising matures, like in the most advanced markets, the user involvement also matures. In Japan today, already 44% of mobile phone owners click on ads they receive on their phones. Mobile advertising was worth 900 million dollars in Japan alone.

According to the research firm, Berg Insight, the global mobile advertising market was estimated to be €1 billion in 2008. Furthermore, Berg Insight forecasts the global mobile advertising market to grow at a compound annual growth rate of 43 percent to €8.7 billion in 2014.

It is my earnest hope and desire that such data will be

made available for Africa, especially Nigeria, the most popu-
lous black nation, so we can maximize this invaluable asset.

Common Types of Mobile Ads

- Mobile Web Banner (top of page)

- Mobile Web Poster (bottom of page banner)

- SMS advertising (which has been estimated at over 90%
  of mobile marketing revenue worldwide).

- MMS advertising,

- Advertising within mobile games

- Advertising within mobile videos, and during mobile TV
  receipt,

- Full-screen interstitials, which appear while a requested
  item of mobile content or mobile web page is loading
  up, and

- Audio advertisements that can take the form of a jingle
  before a voicemail recording, or an audio recording
  played while interacting with a telephone-based service
  such as movie ticketing or directory assistance.

How to Measure the Effectiveness
of Mobile Ad Campaigns

The effectiveness of a mobile media ad campaign
can be measured in a variety of ways. The main measure-
ments are

- **Views (Cost per Impression):** the number of times
  target customers view the ad campaign.

- **Click-through (Cost Per Click):** this involves the target clicking on the ad; he may or may not make a buying decision eventually

- **Click-to-call rates:** this involves the target clicking the ad, and eventually making a decision either to call for more information, or actually making a buying decision.

- **Cost per Install (CPI)** where there the pricing model is based on the user installing an App on their mobile phone. CPI Mobile Advertising Networks work either as incent or non-incent. In the incent model the user is given virtual points or rewards to install the game or App.

SMS Marketing

This is marketing that is done through mobile phones' SMS (Short Message Service). It became increasingly popular in the early 2000s in Europe and other parts of the world when businesses started to collect mobile phone numbers and send off wanted (or unwanted) content.

On average, SMS messages are read within four minutes, making them highly convertible.

Mobile Commerce

The phrase mobile commerce was originally coined in 1997 to mean "the delivery of electronic commerce capabilities directly into the consumer's hand, anywhere, via wireless technology." It is the use of wireless handheld devices such as cellular phones and laptops to conduct commercial transactions online.

Mobile commerce transactions continue to grow, and

the term includes the purchase and sale of a wide range of goods and services, online banking, bill payment, information delivery and so on. It is also known as m-commerce.

According to BI Intelligence in January 2013, 29% of mobile users have now made a purchase with their phones. Wal-Mart estimated that 40% of all visits to their internet shopping site in December 2012 was from a mobile device. Bank of America predicts $67.1 billion in purchases will be made from mobile devices by European and U.S. shoppers in 2015. Mobile retailers in UK alone are expected to increase revenues up to 31% in 2013–14.

Common Products and Services Available

The commonest products and services available via the mobile commerce include (but not limited to) the following:

- **Mobile Money Transfer:** this generally refers to payment services operated under financial regulations and performed from or via a mobile device. Instead of paying with cash, cheque, or credit cards, a consumer can use a mobile phone to pay for a wide range of services and digital or hard goods. Common mobile payment platforms in Nigeria include MyPesa, Paga, M-Teller, M-Naira, VTN, M-Wallet, Monitise, Access Mobile, Enterprise Mobile, Diamond Mobile, SwipeMax Wallet, Breeze Nigeria, Sterling Mobile, Wema Verve, EaZyMoney, QuickTeller, etc.

- **Mobile ATM:** The mobile ATM device easily attaches to most Smartphones and dispenses money instantly and effortlessly– forever ending your search for the nearest bank or ATM. Just type in your personal pin code on your cell phone and access all your cash from the palm of your hand.

- **Mobile ticketing:** This is the process whereby customers can order, pay for, obtain and validate tickets from any location and at any time using mobile phones or other mobile handsets. Mobile tickets reduce the production and distribution costs connected with traditional paper-based ticketing channels and increase customer convenience by providing new and simple ways to purchase tickets.

- **Mobile vouchers, coupons and loyalty cards:** Mobile ticketing technology can also be used for the distribution of vouchers, coupons, and loyalty cards. These items are represented by a virtual token that is sent to the mobile phone. A customer presenting a mobile phone with one of these tokens at the point of sale receives the same benefits as if they had the traditional token. Stores may send coupons to customers using location-based services to determine when the customer is nearby.

- **Content purchase and delivery:** Currently, mobile content purchase and delivery mainly consists of the sale of ring- tones, wallpapers, and games for mobile phones. The convergence of mobile phones, portable audio players, and video players into a single device is increasing the purchase and delivery of full-length music tracks and video. The download speeds available with 4G networks make it possible to buy a movie on a mobile device in a couple of seconds.

- **Location-based services:** Location-based services

(LBS) are a general class of computer program-level services that use location data to control features. As such LBS is an information service and has a number of uses in social networking today as an entertainment service, which is accessible with mobile devices through the mobile network and which uses information on the geographical position of the mobile device. This has become more and more important with the expansion of the Smartphone and tablet markets as well.

The location of the mobile phone user is an important piece of information used during mobile commerce or m- commerce transactions. Knowing the location of the user allows for location-based services such as:

- Local discount offers
- Local weather
- Tracking and monitoring of people
- **Information services:**A wide variety of information services can be delivered to mobile phone users in much the same way as it is delivered to PCs. These services include:
  - News
  - Stock quotes
  - Sports scores
  - Financial records
  - Traffic reporting

Customized traffic information, based on a user's actual travel patterns, can be sent to a mobile device. This customized data is more useful than a generic traffic- report broadcast, but was impractical before the invention of modern mobile devices due to the bandwidth requirements.

- **Mobile Banking:** Banks and other financial institutions use mobile commerce to allow their customers to access account information and make transactions, such as purchasing stocks, remitting money. This service is often referred to as Mobile Banking, or M-Banking.

- **Mobile brokerage:** Stock market services offered via mobile devices have also become more popular and are known as Mobile Brokerage. They allow the subscriber to react to market developments in a timely fashion and irrespective of their physical location.

- **Auctions:** Over the past three years mobile reverse auction solutions have grown in popularity. Unlike traditional auctions, the reverse auction (or low-bid auction) bills the consumer's phone each time they place a bid. Many mobile SMS commerce solutions rely on a one-time purchase or one-time subscription; however, reverse auctions offer a high return for the mobile vendor as they require the consumer to make multiple transactions over a long period of time.

- **Mobile browsing:** Using a mobile browser - a World Wide Web browser on a mobile device - customers can shop online without having to be at their personal computer.

- **Mobile purchase:** Catalog merchants can accept orders from customers electronically, via the customer's mobile device. In some cases, the merchant may even deliver the catalog electronically, rather than mailing a paper catalog to the customer. Some merchants provide mobile websites that are customized for the smaller screen and limited user interface of a mobile device.

- **In-application mobile phone payments:** Payments can be made directly inside of an application running on a popular Smartphone operating system, such as Google Android. Analyst firm Gartner expects in-application purchases to drive 41 percent of app store (also referred to as mobile software distribution platforms) revenue in 2016.

In-app purchases can be used to buy virtual goods, new and other mobile content and is ultimately billed by mobile carriers rather than the app stores themselves. Ericsson's IPX mobile commerce system is used by 120 mobile carriers to offer payment options such as try- before-you-buy, rentals and subscriptions.

Email marketing

This is directly marketing a commercial message to a group of people using email. In its broadest sense, every email sent to a potential or current customer could be considered email marketing. It usually involves using email to send ads, request business, or solicit sales or donations, and is meant to build loyalty, trust, or brand awareness.

Types of Email Marketing

- **Transactional emails:** These are emails sent to clients with whom you have some form business transactions.

The purpose of these emails is to facilitate, complete, or confirm a commercial transaction that the recipient has previously agreed to enter into with the sender, along with a few other narrow definitions of transactional messaging. Triggered transactional messages include dropped basket messages, password reset emails, purchase or order confirmation emails, order status emails, reorder emails and email receipts.

- **Direct emails:** This involves sending an email solely to communicate a promotional message (for example, an announcement of a special offer or a catalogue of products).

- **Opt-in emails:** This is also known as permission marketing. It is a method of email marketing where the recipient has already consented to receive it, either by direct or indirect subscriptions. Under this type of marketing, the recipient is always anticipating the email. This is mainly because the content of the email is somewhat relevant to her personal or business development.

Uses of Email Marketing

There are three (3) basic uses of email marketing. They include:

1. Sending email messages with the purpose of enhancing the relationship of a merchant with its current or previous customers, to encourage customer loyalty and repeat business.

2. Sending email messages with the purpose of acquiring new customers or convincing current customers to pur-

chase something immediately.

3. Adding advertisements to email messages sent by other companies to their customers.

How to Generate Lists of Email Clients

1. Keep a blog where people can have access to information that will help them become better in their life endeavours. You can then make them fill a form where they can subscribe for updates or newsletters.

2. You can give free materials that people will be interested in, but let them subscribe via email where you can send them a download link.

3. You can also rent (or buy) email addresses from service companies that offer such services.

Factors to Consider for Effective Email Marketing Campaigns

I. Pricing: People have a lot of messages and other activities competing for their attention. What will attract them to read and respond to your email will be your pricing offering. Make sure your price is competitive and reasonable enough for people to want to make a commitment to your services.

II. Duration: When you give a bonus, specify when the offering opens and when it closes. Be keen on how long the discount opens for subscription. Make it short enough so as to generate more sales.

III. Flexibility: Be flexible in your method of reply. It shouldn't necessarily be that your recipients must also reply you by email. Include your phone number, toll-free lines, social media or chat room id like BlackBerry Messenger, Whatsapp, Twitter, etc

PRINCIPLES OF MOBILE MILLIONAIRES

There are quite some principles that the mobile millionaire adopts. Knowing and practicing these principles has made me a big player in the mobile world.

These principles include:

The Principle of Simplicity:

This principle states that whatever you do on the internet, especially with mobile technology, it must be easy enough for even the least educated person to use. Whenever I consider this principle, I think of www.google.com. The search engine is so easy that every Jack can use it.

The Principle of Cross-Platform:

This principle states that all your offerings, especially

websites and apps, must be designed to work on every available device. Take for example a website. Design your websites bearing in mind that not everyone will view it from a PC (computer). You must then ensure that whatever the device, visitors to your website will not have any issues viewing and navigating through the pages.

The Principle of Complexity:

This principle is also called The Power of More. It states that you must be willing to offer more than the users deserve. Do not hold back anything from your users. Whatever it is you are offering - a product, service (as discussed in previous chapters), or an app, give your intended users more.

The Principle of Customer-Centeredness:

This principle states that you must work with your target customer or client in mind. It is not about what you like. It is about what your customer needs. No matter how bright your idea, no matter how brilliant your offering, if it does not meet the needs and aspirations of your clients, it will all be a waste.

While writing this book, I had a challenge with one of my web designers. He had this beautiful concept about a particular website he developed for me, the website was beautiful, the concept was great, he was so enthusiastic about it, but my clients all complained that they had difficulties navigating the website. The concept was great but it did not meet my needs. Do not try this with your clients.

The Principle of Niche:

This principle states that every offering must have a clearly marked-out audience in view. Do not try to be everything to everybody. Do not try to be a jack-of-all-trades. If, for example, you are composing a message for email marketing, have a target in view. Not everyone will be interested in your offering - no matter how appealing. But you can tailor your message to get the attention of your intended audience. If you don't, your message will be too watery to attract any response.

The Principle of Creativity:

This principle states that you must be different to make a difference. People are used to the ordinary, general, as usual offerings. Give your clients some reasons to think you are crazy. Do something unique and a bit out of this world. Wow your clients - while not breaking the other principles. They will respect you for your creativity and be willing to pay for your services - even more than you deserve.

The Principle of Visibility:

This principle states that your positioning determines your profiting. You must know how to position yourself via marketing. No matter how great what you are offering is, if people don't know about it, you are like a handsome guy winking at a lady in the dark: there will be no response. You are doing something only you know about.

POWER OF THE MOBILE

A billion mobile subscribers were added in the last four years leaving the total users of mobile communications standing at 3.2 billion - almost half the world's population. Mobile technology (and devices) form a critical part of innovation technology, which in the 21st century is referred to as the 'Third Platform'. These mobile (or Smart) devices - portable tools that connect to the internet - have become a part of our lives.

In the last quarter of 2010, sales of smart phones outpaced those of PCs for the first time, according to data from IDC. By 2014, more smart devices could be used to access the internet than traditional computers. There is an obvious move to an increasingly mobile world, and this is creating new players and new opportunities for a variety of industries.

Based on statistics, over the next four years, the number of people accessing the Internet through PCs will shrink by 15 million as the number of mobile users increases by 91 million. In 2015, there will be more consumers accessing the Internet through mobile devices than through PCs.

Critical Facts About The Mobile World

The picture below gives a graph of the total world population connected to a mobile device.

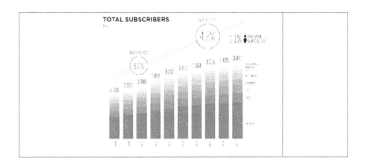

Source: GSMA Wireless Intelligence

Emerging markets will also create plenty of opportunities related to smart technology, and this will not be limited to for-profit enterprises.

This will not be limited to for-profit enterprises. As smart devices become increasingly accepted, companies are also moving into adjacent markets to exploit new revenue models such as mobile commerce (m-commerce) and mobile payment systems. It should be noted that a number of data and tech giants are already jockeying for position in this area.

This growth is mirrored by strong mobile connections growth, to almost 7 billion connections in 2012, as many consumers have multiple devices or use multiple SIMs to access the best tariffs, while firms in many industry sectors roll out M2M applications to boost their own productivity and tap into new markets.

Despite challenging economic headwinds in many regions, the market is expected to grow even more strongly on the dimension of connections over the next five years, with 3 billion additional connections expected to be added between 2012 and 2017, a growth rate of 7.6% p.a. The figure below gives the number of active mobile networks subscribers all over the world:

Benefits Of Mobile Technology

1. Reductions in cost of managing health information systems. In Kenya, for example, mobile phones are being

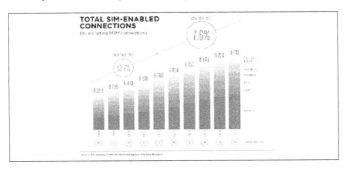

used to collect data and report on disease-specific issues from more than 175 health centres serving over 1 million people. This technology has reduced the cost of the country's health information system by 25% and cut the time needed to report the information from four weeks to one week.

2. Mobile devices give individuals constant access to information, regardless of location, anytime.

3. They also provide broad social benefits such as remote access to education and health care information.

4. Smart devices help to trigger an information explosion that blurs the traditional boundaries within, and across, industries.

5. It empowers consumers and provides new and huge opportunities for businesses. It should be noted, however, that mobile technology also poses a disruptive threat to businesses and individuals that cannot flow with this trend.

Opportunities Provided By Mobile Technology

1. Given this dynamism, it is no surprise that the mobile industry makes a substantial economic contriution, with mobile operators alone expected to contribute 1.4% to global GDP in 2012 and their revenues expected to grow at a robust 2.3% p.a. to reach US$1.1 trillion by 2017. When the rest of the mobile ecosystem is included, total revenues are

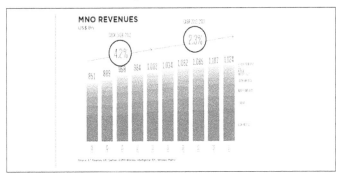

forecast by A. T. Kearney to reach US$2 trillion in 2017, which represents an annual growth rate of 4.7%. In support of the growth in capacity and the level of innovation, the mobile ecosystem will increase its level of annual capital expenditure by just under 4% per annum from 2012 to 2017 to US$238 billion.

2. Mobile infrastructure is now as important to a country's economy as its energy grid or transportation network – it is a key enabling infrastructure that drives and supports growth in the wider economy. A high level of investment is needed to continue the development of this infrastructure so that capacity can be built to meet the ever growing demand and so that new services can be launched which bring greater benefits to the wider economy.

3. The mobile industry has always made a significant contribution to public funding. By 2017, its contribution to public funding is projected to be US$550 billion – as a result of spectrum fees as well as direct and indirect taxes. It is important that this level of financial commitment should be structured in a fair and predictable manner, in order to protect growth and employment – for instance the industry already supports 8.5 million jobs today and growth is expected in emerging markets to create an additional 1.3 million jobs by 2017.

4. The mobile industry is working to support and protect citizens. From empowering women or protecting the vulnerable to helping responses to natural and man-made disasters, mobile phones have significant potential to change the lives of millions. But with any new technology comes new

risks and the whole mobile ecosystem is collaborating to reduce risks to users such as handset theft, mobile fraud and breach of privacy.

Mobile operators are also playing their part to work to reduce their impact on the environment and have the potential to make a net positive impact on greenhouse gas emissions – with the potential to enable emission savings in 2020 more than 11 times greater than their own anticipated mobile network emissions.

Across all of these areas, the GSMA is leading the drive to implement innovative new services and implement robust protective measures through the sharing of best practices and by encouraging inter and intra-industry co-operation.

5. Social Media. There are more than 680 million active monthly mobile users on Facebook, 120 million active monthly mobile users on Twitter, 40 million active monthly mobile users on Foursquare, and 46 million active monthly mobile users on LinkedIn.

6. Increased phone engagements. An average individual spends daily 25 minutes on the internet, 17 minutes on the social media, 16 minutes doing music, 14 minutes on games, 12 minutes on calls, 11 minutes on emails, 10 minutes on SMS, 9 minutes watching video, 9 minutes reading books, and 3 minutes taking or watching pictures, all with the advent of Smartphone combined with the widespread deployment of mobile broadband networks.

Hindrances To Being
Connected To The Mobile Web

There are still many adults and young people who would appreciate the social and economic benefits of mobile technology but are unable to access it, highlighting a huge opportunity for future growth and a challenge to all players in the industry ecosystem to expand the scope of products and services to tap this demand. Some of the easily identified hindrances to being connected to the web include: -

- **Expensive devices:** In many developing countries, due to a high poverty rate, some of the population consider these devices as too expensive.

- **Expensive service plans:** For some others, the service plans are simply unaffordable.

- **Poor mobile network:** Mobile networks are usually better in city centres. In suburbs, there are rarely no mobile networks to connect to.

- **Content isn't available in the local language.**

- **An awareness of the value of the internet is limited.**

- **Availability of power sources is limited.**

- **Networks can't support large amounts of data.**

General Guidelines
For Becoming A Mobile Millionaire

Got all the tools you need to begin using your device for more productive functions? Here are a few lesson you need to learn. - Identify your strengths, and work on them. Mobile Millionaires don't do things they are not good at. They focus on their strengths and delegate their weaknesses.

Have a plan. Don't just breeze in to the mobile (or internet) world aimlessly. If you don't have a roadmap, you will soon lose your way to others who know why they are here.

Fail forward. You will make mistakes and do things that will not work. But it is insanity to make the same mistakes twice. Fail. Learn. And move forward. Be better today than you were yesterday.

Be tenacious. Don't think people will just make way for you because you have a foolproof idea. You can take my word for this; you will be kicked and tossed around till you can stand your ground. You must then make up your mind that it is not over till you win. Winners are losers who refuse to quit.

Be consistent. You must always be in the face of the people. Once you begin, hang in there till you win. Don't undulate. Don't be away today, back tomorrow. Be predictable (that you will always be there).

Be compassionate. Be genuinely interested in meeting the needs of your clients. Stay through with them till you solve their problems. Compassion is the only guarantee for expansion. The more compassionate you are, the more attracted and connected you are to your clients. - Be prompt. Be swift. Let your service delivery be unbeatable - in terms of speed and quality. The faster your delivery, the more jobs you can take on, the more money you make. Riches answer to volume of businesses done within the shortest space possible.

MY EXPERIENCE WITH MOBILE TECHNOLOGY

Reading this title would usually create one of two reactions in the mind of the reader: Either you would believe it's possible, and desire to replicate it, or you would be curious and want to read this further. Whatever your reason, this is REAL! And I will show you how you too can duplicate same success story.

HOW I MADE N3.5 MILLION IN TWO WEEKS
(This is especially targeted to the Nigerian market)

First, I would like to reveal my reasons for wanting to share this with you.

1) I never would have thought this would be possible,

until I bought a book from a respected Author: Ayo Arowolo. It was sent with a little eBook titled, *'HOW I MADE N2MILLION IN TWO WEEKS.'* The secrets I learnt from that book helped me make more money today. If it worked for me, it can work for you.

2) My most respected coach and Mentor, Bishop Oyedepo once shared with his protégé why he devoted time to mentor him. 'A Footballer who does not retire to become a coach will soon pay to enter the same stadium others watched him play. But if he retires to become a coach, when a reigning star he mentored scores, the star will point at him and say 'Coachy!' That way, he never loses relevance. By sharing this, I hope to remain relevant and share in your joy when you duplicate my success, and even surpass it.

3) I was born poor within a suburb in Maiduguri. I was so poor that I made a vow to help people if God ever blessed me. For over six years, I have been involved in paying the tuition of orphans and organizing events to impact their lives. I have also organized hundreds of seminars and conferences in different states in Nigeria to empower people for financial freedom.

The above reasons and more are grounds for sharing this.

To learn more about me you can go to the following links:

Nigerian Communication Week. Click link to read: *http://bit.ly/PK846J*

Nigerian Tribune Newspaper. Click link to read: *http://bit.ly/QOEIFs*

Now, let us begin the journey to multiple streams of income. An eBook by Ayo Arowolo inspired me in my quest for making millions in few weeks. Weeks before I bought those materials I had started experiencing challenges in business. I had a good office in the centre of Lagos; Ikeja. A good location. I had invested over N2million in just two months, and nothing came in; yet Ayo Arowolo made that same amount in weeks. I had to learn from him.

Worthy of note is the fact that I also had a few investments and was in huge debt. Our business was still bringing in little, but I needed to make far more so as to be able to clear my debts, and become a multi-millionaire.

What did I do?

I got a book written by a protégé, after being trained by him on a course he offered. With his permission, I started selling his course. The title was *HOW TO MAKE OVER N200,000 MONTHLY FROM IMPORTATION BUSINESS*. I was selling it at first for 7,500 without any paid adverts, and made over N100,000 but that wasn't my dream. I wanted to make far more.

I soon discovered information is the most purchased commodity in the world. Social Media is information. Everything you see on earth is riding on the wings of information. Your rising and falling is a function of the information at your disposal.

Here in Nigeria, there are some notable Internet Marketers too who have made good money from information marketing, through which they have also established great businesses for themselves. Information business is a huge career, and one thing unique about it is that, it requires little or no money to start; all you need is the inspiration and the know-how.

The revenue in the business is so huge that you can make between N500, 000 to N1, 000,000 within a week if you get your combinations right. Information marketing business is a business for smart people. If you can get smart with your ideas, you are surely going to make quick money in this business. Others have done it and are still doing it. So why can't you?

Sunny Obazu Ojeagbase

The Chairman of Complete Communications Ltd, Publishers of Complete Sports Newspaper, Success Digest Daily, and Complete Football. He is one of the pioneers of the Information marketing revolution in Nigeria. He actually built his multimillion Naira publishing business empire said to be worth more than N600Million through information marketing.

Akin Alabi

Though I have not had a personal encounter with him, I've seen and heard a lot about his Information marketing exploits. He is one guy whose selling skills and tactics I admire very much. A very talented information marketer and copywriter. Mr. Alabi built his sports betting company and other businesses (currently worth hundreds of millions according to my estimate) purely with the money he made from Information Marketing.

Oluwafisayo Akinlolu

I used to be a subscriber to his newsletter in those

days and got really inspired by his articles. He too is into information marketing, and was very popular in the *Success Digest* magazine before it became free for all. His Hulk Group of Companies was conceived and delivered through the information marketing business.

These are just few people I can think of at the moment. There are so many successful Nigerian Information Marketers (too numerous to be mentioned here) who through information marketing have created wealth, legitimate wealth, for themselves.

This business is so simple you can do it with your eyes closed and your hands tied behind your back. If you really want to start a profitable business straight away without going on your knees begging for funding, go with *INFORMATION MARKETING.* But what really is Information Marketing? Just as the name goes, Information Marketing is the act of providing useful information to information seekers with the aim of helping them solve their problems while making money in return.

The internet has become the fastest medium for getting information on just about anything; and millions of people are turning to it every day to get information. If you have any useful information about anything these people are looking for, you can market it to them and make money - millions!

Let's put it this way. Every day, five hundred thousand people are looking for information through Google on the internet about how to lose weight, if you have any useful information on how anyone can lose weight and package it in any format - eBook, DVD, Audio, etc – you will find people would be willing and ready to buy it from you at any reasonable price.

If you sell to just 1,000 persons at N2,000 each, you'll make 2000x1000 =N2,000,000 and you can achieve this in no time if you are good at the business. Can you now see the reason Information Marketing has been called the multimillion dollars business?

So the question is not whether there is money in information marketing, the real question should be how to get it right.

One specific area of information I market is email and phone number databases. With products ranging from N55,000 to N450,000 per data, making a lot of cash is not just a dream but a reality. All you need is 50-200 clients and you are in Millions.

Below is a product I advertised and sold that raked in N3.5million in just two weeks. I have pasted it exactly as I listed it in the advert with no changes whatsoever:

'GILEADBALM GROUP (A LEADING DIGITAL MARKET-ING FIRM IN AFRICA) is registered with the Nigeria Corporate Affairs Commission (CAC), with Reg. No. 150404. Gilead-BalmGroup is a Lagos Based Digital Marketing Company that offers Professional Website Design | Social Media Marketing | Search Engine Optimization | Internet Advertising | Mobile Marketing | Online Reputation Management | Web and Mobile Application Development | Bulk SMS | Mobile Messaging |

Get 50% discount on all our products and services, THIS MEANS THE PRICES BELOW HAVE BEEN REDUCED BY HALF,

AND WILL INCREASE MORE THAN 100% AFTER THE PROMO.

It Is Extended to Friday 24th OCTOBER.

Get the Most Complete GSM Database classified by (Name ,SEX, LGA) for the whole Country. 100% Satisfaction guaranteed. Each LGA for N100,000. Each State for N200,000 and Nationwide for N450,000. This is only available for two weeks. After that, Each is N500,000 and each State is N1million and nationwide is N2million.

- 10,000 business Directory (Email, Phone number & Addresses)- N30,000

- Ikeja Business Owner Directory (7000 GSM Numbers)- N20,000

- General nationwide 1.5million email addresses for- N55,000

- Jamb Writer Database- N150,000

- Get 50,000 email addresses and 50,000 phone numbers of senior and cooperate executives-N55,000

- 880,000 working class email-N55,000

- N2 million Lagosians: email addresses – N85,000

- Make a monthly income of over N1million venturing into bulk SMS business. Simply start with a reseller website for a Promo offer of N15,000 instead of N35,000naira.

- We have a new database of Car owners, Politicians, Online users, Real estate Agents, Civil Servants, Job seekers, Telecoms staff, Cable satellite subscribers and travellers up to 18,913,625.

This is the information most of you have been asking for;

Database, Location, Description, Quantity.

1. Registered Businesses Nationwide Numbers of businesses in Nigeria **8,586,345**

2. Lagos Island Residents Lagos people living/working on the island **375,784**

3. Car owners Nationwide people who have cars **4,290,743**

4. Politicians Nationwide Active politicians & office holders **1,367,345**

5. Online Users nationwide People who use the internet often **635,734**

6. Real estate Agents Nationwide People who deal in properties **65,807**

7. Civil Servants Lagos Civil & public servants **26,780**

8. Job Seekers Nationwide people looking for jobs **335,354**

9. Telecoms Staffs Nationwide People working with diff telecoms **8,983**

10. Cable Satellite Subscribers Nationwide People who subscribe for cable TV **332,368**

11. Travellers Nationwide people who travel or likely to **2,678,382**

TOTAL: 18,913,625   PRICE: N250,000

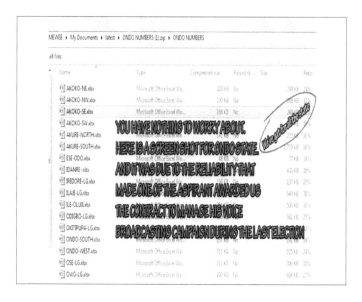

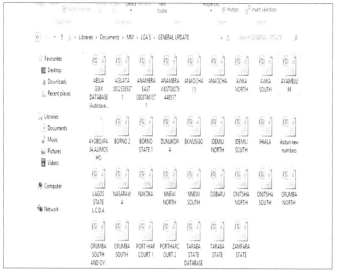

11) 70,000 NUMBERS OF HIGH NETWORTH INDIVIDUALS FOR N80,000 only

11) 70,000 NUMBERS OF HIGH NETWORTH INDIVIDUALS FOR N80,000 only

12) 110,000 numbers of politicians and civil servants for N80,000

Call: (+234) 803 942 4917, 803 267 8670

BBPin: 7F3C535F, 79F29756.

TO ORDER:

PAY PRICE AMOUNT TO GTBANK, GILEADBALM, 0050464651. AND TEXT OR CALL 08039424917 WITH YOUR PAYMENT DETAILS AND EMAIL ADDRESS, AND WE WILL FORWARD IT TO YOU IMMEDIATELY.'

That was all I posted. And the results were astounding.

When it comes to information marketing, what you are selling is information. Information that is in the format of EBooks, Audios, Videos, Seminars, software etc. So, for example, if you are good at helping people solve relationship problems, you can write an E-book or create an audio or even record a video series, package it and sell it. I am not the only one selling *GSM AND EMAIL* Databases but I made far more than most colleagues.

Why?

1) I carried out a research determine if email marketing and sales of database was illegal in Nigeria. At the moment it isn't.

2) I also carried out a research to know if the Nigerian market needed such products. I got a positive response. This got me running.

Do you know?

- Over 80% of Nigerian mobile phone users have seen an SMS advert on their phones.

- Over 55% responded by sending an SMS message back, the most popular ad response.

- Over 60% recalled seeing an SMS advert in the past 30 days and say they responded in some way, according to our recent research.

- Over 1 billion SMS messages are sent by Nigerians per Year.

Any individual, institution or organization in Nigeria

that fails to evolve with the ongoing SMS marketing revolution in the country will sooner or later be out of touch with Nigerians. This is simply because there are over 90 million GSM phone users and the list is growing.

Therefore, there's no other more effective means of reaching Nigerians in their millions than through their phones. And this trend is not going to stop any time soon even if there's adequate supply of electricity in the country to power our radios and TVs because people hardly carry them around.

But the GSM phone is the next most important item in people's bags, purses or pockets.

Why use SMS?

Why not use radio, TV or newspaper for my advertisement?

Current Statistics

* *11% of Nigerians watch TV daily*

* *26% of Nigerians listen to radio daily*

* *6% of Nigerians read newspapers daily*

* *Less than 2% of Nigerians use the internet daily*

* *55% of Nigerians use their mobile phone daily and, most importantly, text Messages have a 96% read rate.*

There are Endless Possibilities with SMS Advertising, and over 100 uses of SMS which you can take advantage of. Your targets:

• **Politicians** - To create awareness for their campaigns and popularity

• **Real Estate Agents** -To advertise properties for

sale/rent

• **Corporate organizations** -To advertise products, Services and Promotions

• **Stores & Supermarkets** -To advertise prize reductions & Sales and boost patronage

• **Churches** - For evangelism

• **Government Ministries, Agencies and Departments** -To announce important government programs to the people. E.g. Tax payment or voters registration.

• **For short code Marketing and Advertising etc.**

Other people who can be reached through bulk SMS Marketing include: Restaurants, Hotels, Cafes, Event Promoters, Concert Promoters, Product Promoters, Newspapers, Magazines, Fm Radio, Cable Networks, Satellite Television, Schools, Colleges, Universities, Political Parties, NGO's, Welfare Organizations , Estate Agents, Real Estate agencies.

Also, any company can send alerts, offers, greetings etc to their clients or suppliers on various festivals or other occasions. Any updates or messages can be sent to employees and clients.

GSM Numbers Database

I ensured I bought the most up-to-date database of all GSM mobile phone numbers in Nigeria. These include GSM and CDMA mobile numbers from all the major networks in Nigeria. Our over-90-million database is highly profiled on a state-by-state basis. Thus, you can target your message to any specific location in Nigeria.

We ensure that whatever your goals are, whether it's to sell, promote, brand, inform, notify, educate or create awareness, you can take advantage of the most cost-effective, direct, targeted, reliable, immediate and instant way to deliver your message to Nigerians in any part of Nigeria.

Gtext.com.ng is also one of my companies, and can provide GSM Numbers in excess of 90million and send your SMS adverts to every GSM number in Nigeria from MTN to Zain, Glo and Etisalat networks. We offer customized bulk SMS marketing and advertising for diverse clients no matter what their budgets are.

Our phone number database is compiled to the highest proximity achievable in the industry.

Email Marketing

Email advertising and marketing has long been on the list of most cost-effective and widespread methods of digital advertising and marketing. Marketing and advertising is an important part of building businesses. It can reach a wider audience in a faster amount of time with little to no cost. One just needs an email address.

Email marketing is not to be confused with spam. However, if not careful, the way the email is written can make it sound like spam, and the user will block any emails from that point forward.

Dear Marketer,

- *Have you wasted so much money advertising your products or service, and pasting your ads with nothing to show for it?*

- *Do you have a product or service to sell?*

- *Are you getting tired of promoting your business and getting nowhere?*
- *Are you interested in increasing your sales by 1000?*
- *Are you sick of only getting counter offers in your inbox?*
- *Are you looking for something with an exceptional difference?*

If you've answered yes to any of these questions then the solution is here. Targeted email is the most direct and powerful method of marketing on the internet today. Targeted, Safe, with a 100% Opt-In!!

Benefits of Email Marketing.

- **Target Marketing**

You can promote the services to the businesses or people that are in the particular market so it won't be bothersome to businesses that aren't associated with yours. - Relationship Building This is email marketing at its most basic level. You can develop relationships with customers through email because more customers like dealing through email. Becoming more personal on the emails also promote the business.

- **Time**

It takes a very short amount to write a marketing campaign and click "Send". You can then devote other resources to marketing because of the time saved.

- **Link Building**

This is a good way to create link building, which is incorporating links to the website or affiliate websites to draw in customers to the site.

71

- **Marketing Outside of Business Hours**

The customers will know what is being marketed even after business hours.

If you are selling any product on the internet or need to market yourself (advertise your products) on the internet, then Bulk Mailing is the fastest approach to achieve your targets. There are potentially millions of targeted Nigerian buyers willing to purchase your product or service.

I branded *gtext.com.ng* as a Nigerian Internet Marketing Company providing quality email Lists. We are committed to providing unique, innovative and cost-effective ways to increase your customer base. Gileadbalm Group is like no other email list provider you will find on the internet. All of our email lists are compiled and updated from the previous week making them the freshest lists available to date.

So, whether you are a small firm planning to sell your products on the internet or a marketer who just wants to advertise products or services on the internet - we have the right lists to get you jumpstarted on the fastest approach to online marketing.

We as a company provide the emails lists you need to start your Bulk Mailing campaign. Buy email lists from us and increase your sales overnight via email marketing.

You can now advertise or market your business, services, events to millions of Nigerians just in a click by purchasing Gileadbalm Group entire 10 Million e-mail address database directory updated weekly which has been proven to bring 100% positive result to several businesses in Nigeria.

We have plans and email lists available to suit each and every pocket with their email marketing needs. Please find below the different options that can be instantly purchased. Simply choose which plan you would like from the list below and make your payment and we will email you your package immediately.

Our fresh email lists will 100% generate you a massive amount of extra traffic to your site. Just watch out for what will happen to your website stats once your campaign is under way using these quality emails!

Just watch out for what will happen to your website stats once your campaign is under way using these quality emails!

***Please note: The only way to make sure that your email campaign is successful is to use a fresh genuine email list ***

Our Exclusive Lists of Nigerian Email Addresses contains: -

- The Highest Quality Opt-In List on the Market

- Freshly Gathered Email Addresses

- Complete email addresses from Nigeria's most active forums and many others. Direct from the owners of the forums (Main webmasters), and also from worldwide sites that accept Nigerians.

So, I've spilled my guts on all I am involved in, what it entails and how I run it.

Now let's get back to you.

What are the tools you need to do the same?

1) GET A Product.

Write up or get a service with resell rights. If you are interested in reselling my phone and email Database, for the Nigerian market, I will give you a special offer for it at the end of this eBook.

2) Package your sales letter.

Listed below are tools you can use to achieve that:

a.) *OpenOffice* – This software is completely free. It's the FREE version of Microsoft Office. If you want to create your e-book, you simply type your e-book (like you type in it Microsoft word). Once you are done, you simply use that same software to convert to PDF; and you have your e-book. You can also use the recent version of Microsoft Office which allows you to save your Microsoft word document in PDF format.

b.) *Camstudio.org* – With this, you can create videos. The videos are recorded live from your computer. You'll only need to use it if you are creating a video product (video tutorials). There are other types of this software you can also use. This part is not compulsory particularly if you are trading in Nigeria.

c.) *Autoresponder* – This is the most important and the heart of your information business. With this autoresponder, you'll be able to build your list of potential customers who will buy your information products. Once you start building your list, you'll then be able to send them emails of good content and also promote your products, etc.

Quite a lot of people like using FREE autoresponders, but I encourage you not to use it. Get *Aweber* or *Getresponse* instead. With just N2,500 per month, you can start using these autoresponders.

d.)**Domain Name & Hosting** – Domain is the address of your website and Hosting is where your website files, etc, are hosted on. The two always go together. With as low as N15,000 per year, you can get hosting and domain name. I can fix this up for you if you want it. All you need is to reach me through the email address at the end of the book.

A lot of people think they can bypass a paid hosting site by using free domains. The truth is, if you are really serious about your own information business, you need to have a domain and hosting. Don't use a FREE one. Many customers will not trust you; and they'll think you are not serious too.

e.) **One-page website design software** – This is the software that you'll use to create your website or blog in the way you want them to look like. For information marketing business purpose, you need to create mini pages or one-page websites. There are various one-page website design softwares. Find the one you can use.

Even if you've never created an information product before, these tools will help you. Take your time, download these tools, play around with them and learn how to use them well if you are ready for your own information business.

3) Make sure you have integrity, and your product has a minimum of 70% accuracy and potency.

4) Get a business name. Some people use individual names but such cannot attract a multinational to do business with you if you are into services like mine.

5) Get a corporate account in a company name. A personal account is not professional and makes you look childish.

6) Get an office or contact address. 95% of my database clients don't come to my office but often ask of the office address. When people are dealing with you with huge cash, they want to be sure you are traceable and touchable.

7) Use Digital Marketing to push your information products. Email marketing and BlackBerry was the most effective marketing methods for me. As a company, we never attracted the big clients until we started email marketing. The era of dropping proposals is long dead because of smartphones. Everyone is able to access their email address instantly and that made email marketing effective.

I can broadcast a sales letter, three times or more, daily on BBM and it works. Viral Facebook campaign, Twitter and Whatsapp are also effective tools of pushing your adverts in order to sell.

With the above, some of you may even make 10million in two weeks. I have already projected higher sales for this, but I may do another eBook after I hit that new sales target. Note that this was personal sales and not that of my company as we have been selling in millions long ago but this was a personal campaign that brought this 100% profit in.

COMPLETE GUIDE TO BULK SMS MARKETING

Here is a clear description of how bulk marketing works.

HOW TO REGISTER AS A NEW USER

To register as a new marketer for bulk SMS, you need to visit the site www.gileadbalmsms.com and follow the instructions below.

Click on Create an account at the left side of the site

• Fill the form that show on the main page

•Note:

• You must not forget your username name because that is what you will use to login into your account.

• Please use a valid email account whose ID and password you are sure of, because your activation link will be sent to the email you provide when filling the form.

• Make sure you fill all the fields provided.

• Click on the 'Register' button.

HOW TO ACTIVATE YOUR ACCOUNT AFTER REGIS-
TRATION

- Open the email you used when filling the registration form on gileadbalm site

- Click on the gileadbalm message in your email box • Click on the activation link which will redirect you back to the gileadbal login page

- Type the username you used when filling the form into the username textbox

- And the password that you provided when filling the form into the password text box

- Click on Login

OR

- After you have clicked on the activation link in your mail

- Type www.gileadbalmsms.com on the address bar of the browser

- Look to the left of the site. You will see the image shown below.

- Type in the username and the password
- Click on 'login'

COMPOSING A MESSAGE

• After logging in you will be redirected to the 'Compose message' area

• SENDER ID: This can be anything either alphabets or numbers but should not be more than 11 characters. It will be the title of the message you are sending.

• RECIPIENTS: This is where you type all the numbers you are sending your message to. Each number must be separated by a comma (,) or semicolon (;). They can all be listed on one column or row.

• MESSAGE: This is where you type the body of the message you intend to send.

NOTE: 159 characters make one page. This count includes white spaces (that is space between the texts).

SMS PRICE LIST

This area displays the prices of SMS units based on the quantity purchased.

MESSAGE HISTORY

This will show you all the previous messages you have sent in case. You may want to reuse the numbers or resend the messages.

LOAD VOUCHER

This is the number generated by the admin of the site which can be use to send messages. It is just like having a unit in your account. If you are given, you will have to put it in the voucher text box and click 'submit'.

PHONE BOOK

You can use this area to create a group where you store phone numbers and members' names group by group.

YOUR TRANSACTION

This area shows the date and amounts of units credited to your account by the Admin.

YOUR SETTING

In this area you can view your personal details and make changes. You can also set your default Sender ID and transfer units from your account to another account.

HOW TO RECOVER A FORGET PASSWORD

• Go to the image shown to the left of the site. Click on 'Forgot your password?'

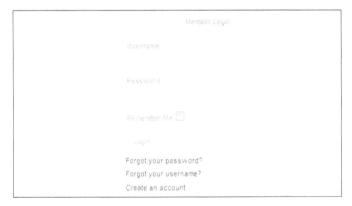

This will come up.

- Type your email address used to register the account
- Click Submit
- After the submission a token will be sent to the email you provided.
- Go and open your mail box to copy the token
- Type your Username
- Paste the token into the token box

- After clicking on 'Submit'
- A new form will appear
- Put un your new password and retype the password in the 'Verify Password' box
- Click Submit

That's it!

In the next section I will like to delve further into how

to use the Admin menu shown below as placed on the *www. gileadbalmsms.com* site.

Generate Vouchers

This is used to generate random numbers to send bulk SMS messages to.

How to Use it

• Specify the number of Vouchers to generate in the 'Total No of Vouchers' to generate textbox'

• Specify the total number of sms units.

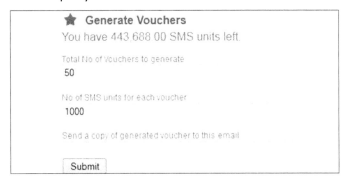

- Specify the email (client email) you are sending vouchers to.

- Click on the Submit Button.

Portal Settings

This section allows the admin of the site to effect price changes per unit, determine number of free units to be given to a new registered member (Gileadbalmsms.com is using

two (2) as you can see bellow), change the API and more. Note: Please if you don't really know what to do in this area contact a technical person to handle this part to avoid errors on your site.

Gateway API:

This connects your site to gileadbalmsms or to any other bulk SMS hosting site. We do not recommend altering it.

✓ GATEWAY API

SMS API Gateway URL

http://api.infobip.com/api/sendsms/plain?user=gilead&password=gilead&sender=@@sender@@&SMSText=@@me

SMS Gateway Response word on Success

0

SMS Gateway URL to check remaining reseller sms

Bulk SMS batch size (default is 50)

100

Permanently disable SMS API Gateway URL modification(Set to yes for your resellers. Once set to yes, it cannot be reversed)

False ▼

COST AND NUMBERS:

This section allow you to change the price range of your SMS unit, Change the currency type and specify the number of characters to make up a one page text message just as your phone does.

✓ COST AND NUMBERS

Selling price per sms unit

```
0-999=2.50
1000-4999=2
5000-9999=1.90
10000-49999=1.50
50000-99999=1.00
100000-499999=0.95
```

Specify country codes that use more that 1 sms unit per text message

```
234817=2
234815=2
234819=1
234818=1.5
234816=2
234813=2
```

Currency symbol

N

Home Country Code e.g 234 if you're in Nigeria

234

Length of 1 sms

160

Length of 1 sms for multiple pages

151

Finally click on the 'Submit' button.

Credit Members:

This section is used to credit the account of all your clients after payment has been confirmed or when you are willing to do so.

To credit a member simply click on 'CREDIT A MEMBER MANUALLY'. Specify the amounts of units to be added (Note: It must be a number -e.g 100, 1000, 20- of your choice).

Click on the drop down box to select the customer's name.

In the 'Send notification' box choose 'Any'. If you choose 'Yes' a notification will be sent to the customer's phone that the customer's account has been credited; but admin will be charged for this from the admin account unit.

Finally click on 'Add Amount.'

Credit Members
u have 443 668 00 SMS units left
APPROVE/CANCEL A TRANSACTION

CREDIT A MEMBER MANUALLY

Specify Amount to Add
Select A Member   "Blessedmum" (Blossom)   ▼
Send Notification   ○ Yes ● No
                         Add Amount

Export Phone Numbers: This section is used to get all

the phone numbers of members and people you or your customer have sent messages to on your site

• I believe you have already clicked on 'Export Phone
Numbers'

• Click on the dropdown menu and select any of the
areas you want to export the numbers from.

Click on the 'Export' button below.

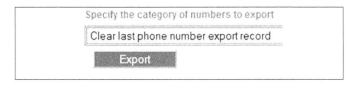

• From the box that opens click on 'OK'.

• Finally click here to download the numbers exported

Manage members: This section allows you to view entire customers that you have on the site, the number of SMS units left in their accounts, and to check all the transactions that the customer has carried out on the site. Just as it is in the diagram below. To view all activities click on 'View detail' on the right.

Manage Sent Messages: This section allows you to view statuses of messages sent to know if they have been sent or are still pending. In this area as well you can delete messages.

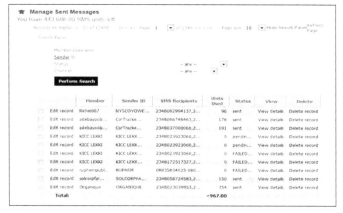

Manage Transactions: This area shows the amounts, SMS units purchased from your seller account and the date.

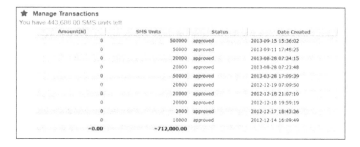

Manage Phonebook: This allows you to edit or delete all or any of your customers from your database.

Manager Vouchers: This section is only useful if you credit your customers using Vouchers. It allows you to view the transactions that all customer have done using vouchers.

HOW TO EDIT ARTICLES

- Login using your admin username and password

- Click on the page you want to edit

- Click on 'Edit article' at the top of the article

- Start to edit the article or add to the article when done.

- To add image to the article click on image at the bottom and browse to the image

- Click on the image
- Click insert to import the image into your article
- Click save

That's it! All the steps needed to get into the information marketing business.

CONCLUSION

A lot has changed since the days Google and Yahoo were just budding search engines. As the technological environment has changed so have the services they offer. This has kept the likes of Google relevant to current trends.

To constantly keep up with the ever-dynamic evolution of the technological landscape, I believe individuals and companies must strive to keep up to date with these trends, as well as being forward thinkers instead of being reactionaries, so as to make it big in mobile technology.

The opportunities of making it big in mobile technology are endless. I just gave you a couple. There is still going to be rapid growth due the fact that most elements of our lives are now centred on these mobile devices. Be it work or play, there is something for everyone.

Consumers and sellers alike are now able to interact without the need of middle-men, so to speak. This means the seller has direct access to rate than traditional sellers. This has opened up the market place, making competition high. This results in better services and prices.

My advice to you at this point? *GET IN WHILE YOU CAN.* Design a product and get it across to the billions of consumers waiting the world over. Remain relevant with the changing landscape. As always, early adaptors will always stay ahead of the chasing pack.

Before I end this, I have decided to give an offer to as many as desire to trade in the same services I did to make N3.5million in two weeks.

All the above Nigerian databases are in excess of N1million under normal rates and we have even stopped the sales of such database as we now send on behalf of client.

However, if you desire to buy all the above database as a reseller, meaning you buy it and resell it at your own price, I will give you all at an amazingly discounted rate; the complete nationwide LGA database and each other database. If you are interested, please contact me through the details listed at the end of the book.

I look forward to seeing you at the top. Feel free to share your testimony with me in my private mail: akintayostephen@yahoo.com.

REFERENCES

- Ernst & Young, 2012. "Tracking global trends: how six key developments are shaping the business world"

- www.internet.org

- GSMA, THE MOBILE ECONOMY 2013

- http://www.businessinsider.com/complete-visual-history-of-cell-phones-2011-5?op=1#ixzz2xGPgO6R4

- ttp://mashable.com/2013/08/05/most-used-smart-phone-apps/

- http://en.wikipedia.org/wiki/Mobile_marketing

- www.visiongain.com

- http://www.jwtintelligence.com/wp-content/uploads/2013/04/F_JWT_13-Mobile-Trends-for-2013-and-Beyond_04.02.13.pdf

ABOUT THE AUTHOR

Stephen Akintayo Is An Inspirational Speaker, Author, Youth Leader, And Entrepreneur. A Digital Marketing Consultant With Various Multinationals In Nigeria, He Is Also The Publisher/Editor-In-Chief Of *CEOPROTEGE MAGAZINE*, A Business Magazine Published By *CEOPROTEGE LIMITED.*

He Is Presently The C.E.O of GILEADBALM GROUP Whose Products And Services Span Different Sectors: Information Technology, Telecom, Marketing, Consulting, Real Estate, Oil And Gas, Agriculture, Etc. He Is Also The President And Founder Of *INFINITY FOUNDATION*, An NGO That Helps Orphans And Less Privileged Children. Infinity Foundation Has Impacted Over 2000 Orphans And Street Children In Africa; With Chapters Spread Across Different Tertiary Institutions In Nigeria And Expanding To Other Schools Across The Globe. The Foundation Also Hosts The Infinity Foundation Charity Award (IFCA), An Individual And Corporate Social Responsibility Award Program.

A Graduate Of Microbiology From Olabisi Onabanjo University, And Member Of The Institute Of Strategic Management, He Is Highly Sought After On TV And Radio.

Having A Vision Of Helping In The Establishment And Growth Of Youths In Every Area Of Their Lives, Stephen Has A Strong Passion To See Undergraduates And Graduates Come Up With Ideas That Will Cause A Business Revolution In Nigeria And AFRICA. His Mentorship Platform Has Helped Thousands In The Area Of Business.

A Relationship Expert And Exceptional Writer, Stephen Akintayo Is Author To Several Bestselling Books Which Include The Mobile Millionaire; Indestructible: Turning Your Mess To Your Message; Soulmates; And Survival Instinct.

He Is An Ordained Pastor With Living Faith Church Worldwide, And Is Happily Married With Two Sons.

———————

CONTACTS:

Telephone: (+234) 8188220077, 8188220066, 08188111999

BBPIN: 5664AD8

Facebook: www.facebook.com/stephenakintayong

Twitter: www.twitter.com/stephenakintayo

Skype: stephenakintayo

Websites: stephenakintayo.com; http://gtext.com.ng;
http://infinityfoundation.org.ng

Email: info@stephenakintayo.com;
Stephenakintayo@gmail.com